First World War
and Army of Occupation
War Diary
France, Belgium and Germany

21 DIVISION
Divisional Troops
237 Machine Gun Company
12 July 1917 - 28 February 1918

WO95/2145/3

The Naval & Military Press Ltd
www.nmarchive.com
Published in association with The National Archives

Published by

The Naval & Military Press Ltd

Unit 10 Ridgewood Industrial Park,

Uckfield, East Sussex,

TN22 5QE England

Tel: +44 (0) 1825 749494

www.naval-military-press.com

www.nmarchive.com

This diary has been reprinted in facsimile from the original. Any imperfections are inevitably reproduced and the quality may fall short of modern type and cartographic standards.

© Crown Copyright
Images reproduced by permission of The National Archives, London, England, 2015.

Contents

Document type	Place/Title	Date From	Date To
Heading	2145/3 237 Machine Gun Company		
Heading	21 Div Troops 237 Machine Gun Coy 1917 Jan-1918 Feb		
War Diary	Belton Park	12/07/1917	12/07/1917
War Diary	Grantham	13/07/1917	13/07/1917
War Diary	Southampton	13/07/1917	13/07/1917
War Diary	Le Havre	14/07/1917	17/07/1917
War Diary	Bois Bur-Au-Mont.	17/07/1917	17/07/1917
War Diary	Moyenneville	18/07/1917	27/07/1917
War Diary	In The Field	01/08/1917	28/08/1917
War Diary	Dainville	01/09/1917	16/09/1917
War Diary	Tauy	17/09/1917	17/09/1917
War Diary	Eecke	18/09/1917	23/09/1917
War Diary	Meleren	28/09/1917	28/09/1917
War Diary	Conqueror Camp	30/09/1917	30/09/1917
War Diary	Scottish Camp	30/09/1917	30/09/1917
War Diary	Anzac Camp	01/11/1917	05/11/1917
War Diary	Hallebast Car	11/11/1917	11/11/1917
War Diary	Dominion Camp	17/11/1917	17/11/1917
War Diary	Vieux Berquin	19/11/1917	19/11/1917
War Diary	Gonnehem	20/11/1917	20/11/1917
War Diary	Hersin	21/11/1917	21/11/1917
War Diary	Mont St Eloy	22/11/1917	30/11/1917
War Diary	Tincourt	01/12/1917	01/12/1917
War Diary	Marquaix	02/12/1917	02/12/1917
War Diary	Hamel	03/12/1917	09/12/1917
War Diary	Line	12/12/1917	12/12/1917
War Diary	Villers Faucon	17/12/1917	17/12/1917
War Diary	Longavesnes	26/12/1917	26/12/1917
War Diary	Villers Faucon	28/12/1917	28/12/1917
War Diary	Saulcourt	31/12/1917	08/02/1918
War Diary	Moislains	09/02/1918	15/02/1918
War Diary	Tincourt	15/02/1918	28/02/1918

2145/3

237 Machine Gun Company

21 DIV TROOPS

237 Machine Gun Coy

1917 JULY — 1918 FEB

237 Divisional M.T. Coy. July 1917   237th Coy M T Coy

Army Form C. 2118.

WAR DIARY
or
INTELLIGENCE SUMMARY.
(Erase heading not required.)

Place	Date	Hour	Summary of Events and Information	Remarks and references to Appendices
Bulls-Wh	12.7.17	11.20pm	Departed for Entraining for Overseas	
Grantham	13.7.17	2.25am	Entrained and left Grantham	
Southampton	13.7.17	10.30am	Arrived at Southampton	
Do	"	6 p.m.	Embarked Southampton for Le Havre	
Le Havre	14.7.17	7.30 am	Arrived Le Havre and disembarked	
Do	"	9.30 am	Coy marched to and arrived at No 1st Rest Camp, Le Havre, at noon and 3 p.m. respectively	
Do	15.7.17	10.0 am	Medical Inspection; also Kit and Anti-Gas Appliances inspected	
Do	16.7.17	7 a.m.	Left Le Havre Rest Camp No 1st	
Do	17.7.17	12.20 am	Entrained Le Havre Station	
Boisleux-au-Mont	17.7.17	1.0 p.m.	Detrained at Boisleux-au-Mont	
Do	"	3.30 p.m.	Left Boisleux-au-Mont and arrived Moyenneville 11.45 p.m. same day and joined 21st Division	
Do				
Moyenneville	18.7.17	11 a.m.	Commanding Officer and two Senior Officers went to "Line" reconnoitring	
Do				

237 Divisional M.G. Coy.

Army Form C. 2118.

WAR DIARY
July 1917.

or

INTELLIGENCE SUMMARY.

(Erase heading not required.)

Instructions regarding War Diaries and Intelligence Summaries are contained in F.S. Regs., Part II. and the Staff Manual respectively. Title pages will be prepared in manuscript.

Place	Date	Hour	Summary of Events and Information	Remarks and references to Appendices
Mazingarbe	19-7-17	2 pm	"A" Section went to "Live" and relieved 62nd Machine Gun Coy.	
"	20-7-17	2 pm	"B" Section went to "Live" and relieved 64th Machine Gun Coy.	
"	21-7-17	12 am	Twelve men of "D" Section under Section Officer went in "Line" for instruction with 110th Machine Gun Coy.	
"	"	2 pm	Twelve men of "C" Section under Section Officer went in "Line" for instruction with 64th Machine Gun Coy.	
"	24-7-17	7 pm	"C" Section returned after short course of instruction	
"	25-7-17	7.15 pm	"D" Section returned after short course of instruction	
"	26-7-17	8 pm	"B" Section returned from "Line" also "A" Section	
"	26-7-17	2 pm	"D" Section went into "Line"	
"	26-7-17	2 pm	"C" Section went into "Line"	
"	27-7-17	2 pm	Twelve men of "A" Section under Section and Sub Section Officers proceeded to "Line" to join 62nd Machine Gun Coy. for instruction in Trench Routine	
"	"	"	Twelve men of "B" Section under Section Officer proceeded to "Live" to join 110th Machine Gun Coy. for instruction in Trench Routine	

A.G. Carey, Capt.
O/C 237 Divisional M.G. Coy.

Army Form C. 2118.

2374th M.G. Coy

Vol 2

237TH COMPANY. M.G.C.
No. 2
Date 1/9/17

WAR DIARY
or
INTELLIGENCE SUMMARY.
(Erase heading not required.)

Instructions regarding War Diaries and Intelligence Summaries are contained in F.S. Regs., Part II. and the Staff Manual respectively. Title pages will be prepared in manuscript.

Place	Date	Hour	Summary of Events and Information	Remarks and references to Appendices
Whitfield	1.8.17	7 hrs	"B" Section Officer and 12 O.R.s arrived at HQ.s from Tenders	
"	"	"	"A" Section and Sub Section Officers and 12 O.R.s arrived at HQ.s from Tenders	
"	5.8.17	2 hrs	"B" Section went in line under Section and Sub Section Officers	
"	"	"	"A" Section went in line under Section and Sub Section Officers	
"	"	"	"C" Section returned from line under Section Officer	
"	"	"	"D" Section returned from line under Section & Sub Section Officers	
"	9.8.17	"	"C" Section went in line under Section Officer	
"	"	"	"D" Section went in line under Section & Sub Section Officers	
"	10.8.17	6 hrs	"A" Section returned from line under Section & Sub Section Officers	
"	12.8.17	9.30 hrs	Water cart slightly damaged by shell fire whilst going to Line	
"	13.8.17	6 hrs	"C" Section went out of line under Section Officer	
"	"	6 p.m.	"A" Section went into line under Section Officer	
"	14.8.17	10 hrs	First fatal casualty of Coy 42953 Pte Sherwood J. being killed	
"	17.8.17	7 hrs	"C" Section went into line under 2nd Lt Frost.	
"	"	"	"D" Section went out of Line under Section and Sub Section Off.	

Army Form C. 2118.

237TH COMPANY. M.G.C.
No.
Date. May 17

WAR DIARY
or
INTELLIGENCE SUMMARY
(Erase heading not required.)

Place	Date	Hour	Summary of Events and Information	Remarks and references to Appendices
Authifield	25.8.17	6 p.m.	"B" Section went in line under 2nd/L Wadsworth.	
"	"	"	"3" Section in out of line under Section Relation Officer.	
"	26.8.17	3 p.m.	"Coy Relieved: Last Gun team arriving at HQrs about 7 a.m. 27.8.17	
"	29.8.17	10.40am	Coy Marched to and arrived at Dainville at 3 p.m.	
"	29/8/17 to 31/8/17		Coy Rest — In Training	

J. Chittenden Lt.
O/C. 237 M.G. Coy

Army Form C. 2118.

WAR DIARY
or
INTELLIGENCE SUMMARY.
(Erase heading not required.)

237th Coy M.G. Coy
Vol 3

Place	Date	Hour	Summary of Events and Information	Remarks and references to Appendices
Dranoutre	1.9.17	—	Coy in training. Divisional Rest.	
do	2.9.17	—	Capt G.H. Beckley rejoined from command of Coy.	
do	8.9.17	—	Coy Other Ranks & 5 Officers, including Capt G.H. Beckley, left for Dickebusch	
do	6.9.17	—	Then to Eecke	
do	16.9.17 9.15 am		Capt A.G. Soper relinquished command of Coy.	
do			Balance of Coy, Coy HQ, Dranoutre and marched to Savy. Arriving Savy 3 pm. "Billeted."	
Savy	17.9.17 2.30 am		Entrained "Savy" 4.30 a.m. — Detrained Caestre, and marched to Eecke arriving at 3.30 pm.	
Eecle	18.9.17	—	Coy in training.	
do	23.9.17	—	Left Eecle 7.15 a.m. Marched to & arrived at Meteren 10 a.m.	
Meteren	25.9.17	—	Left Meteren 12 noon — marched to and arrived at Conqueror Camp at 2.15 pm.	
Conqueror Camp	30.9.17 12.15 pm		Coy marched from "Conqueror Camp" to "Scottish Camp" under Capt G.H. Beckley arriving at 5 pm.	
Scottish Camp	30.9.17 9.30 pm		"A" Section under Section & Sub Section officers and "D" Section under Section officer, Commanded by Capt G.H. Beckley went into line.	

G.H. Beckley
for OC 237th M.G. Coy

Army Form C. 2118.

237th Coy M.G.Corps

WAR DIARY
or
INTELLIGENCE SUMMARY.
(Erase heading not required.)

Place	Date	Hour	Summary of Events and Information	Remarks and references to Appendices
Anzac Camp	1.11.17	—	In line	
do	2.11.17		Out of line	
do	3-5.11.17 noon		Marched to Halloluck Corner — In training	
do	6.11.17	do	Marched to Dominion Camp to do	
Halleluct Cor	7-10.11.17		Dominion Camp for Views Bergen by march-route	
Dominion Camp	11.17.17	do	Left Dominion Camp for Views Bergen by march-route	
Views Bergen	19.11.17 8 am	do	Left Views Bergen for Gonnehem by do	
Gonnehem	20.11.17	do	Left Gonnehem for Herein by do	
Herein	21.11.17 3pm		Left Herein by march-route for Lancaster Camp "Mont St Eloy" for training	
Mont St Eloy	22.11.17		Reconnoitring Area Sector and Training and equiping Coy	
do	30.11.17 10pm		Left for say by March-route and entrained for Vincent	

Joseph E. Enright
O.C. 237 Coy M.G.C.

Army Form C. 2118.

237th Coy MGC

WAR DIARY
or
INTELLIGENCE SUMMARY
(Erase heading not required.)

Dec 1917

Instructions regarding War Diaries and Intelligence Summaries are contained in F. S. Regs., Part II. and the Staff Manual respectively. Title pages will be prepared in manuscript.

Place	Date	Hour	Summary of Events and Information	Remarks and references to Appendices
Lincourt	1-12-17	2 pm	Coy arrived at Lincourt and marched to Marquay	
Marquay	2-12-17	12 noon	Coy marched to and arrived at Daruel at about 5 pm.	
Daruel	3-12-17		Coy in Transport and Reserve	
Daruel	9-12-17		Coy went into line Transport lines near H.Q's Villers Faucon	
Line	12-12-17		Two casualties this day 20674 Pte Binnie W & 98522 Pte Turner R. being	
			injured and wounded by shell fire.	
Villers Faucon	17-12-17		Coy out of line and H.Q's and camps at Longavesnes.	
Longavesnes	26-12-17		Coy marched up into line Transport lines and rear H.Q's at Villers Faucon	
Villers Faucon	28-12-17		Transport and rear H.Q's moved up to Saulcourt	
Saulcourt	31-12-17		Coy in line Transport lines and rear H.Q's Saulcourt	

A.D.L [signature]
OC 237 Coy MGC

A6945 Wt. W1142/M1160 350,000 12/16 D. D. & L. Forms/C/2118/14.

WAR DIARY or INTELLIGENCE SUMMARY

Army Form C. 2118.

237th Coy M.G.C.

237TH COMPANY, M.G.C.

Vol 7

Place	Date	Hour	Summary of Events and Information	Remarks and references to Appendices
Jaulzy	1/1/18	-	Coy in Lines	
do	3/1/18	-	Coy in Lines. Lt. J.E. Enright took over temporary command	
do	4/1/18	-	Coy out of lines this day with exception of 2 gun teams	
do	13/1/18	-	Coy entered line this day commanded by Lt. J.E. Enright	
do	15/1/18	-	H. Cavallier this day 98160 A/Cpl Dickie G. 14634 Pte Sutcliffe J.	
do	do	-	6047 Pte Montgomery D. and 10866 Pte Warwick J. being	
do	do	-	Killed in Action.	
do	21/1/18	-	Coy out of line this day with exception of 2 gun teams	
do	24/1/18	-	Coy entered line this day commanded by Capt. S.I. Chittenden	
do	31/1/18	-	Coy in line	

Joseph E. Enright
2nd Lieut 237 Coy MGC

Army Form C. 2118.

WAR DIARY
INTELLIGENCE SUMMARY.
(Erase heading not required.)

"D" Coy 20th Bn MGC

Place	Date	Hour	Summary of Events and Information	Remarks and references to Appendices
Saulcourt	1/2/18	-	Coy in huts	
	7.2.18	7.30pm	Coy out of line	
Saulcourt	8.2.18	1.30pm	Coy marched to and arrived at Moislains 4.40pm	
Moislains	9.2.18	-	Coy in training	
to	15.2.18	10.30am	Coy left Moislains for Lincourt arriving 1.30pm	
Lincourt	15.2.18	-	Coy in training	
"	26.2.18	-	G.O.C. inspected transport at Demuil	
"	28.2.18	-	Coy preparing for line	

February 1918

J.H. Littleton Capt.
O.C. "D" Coy 20th Bn MGC